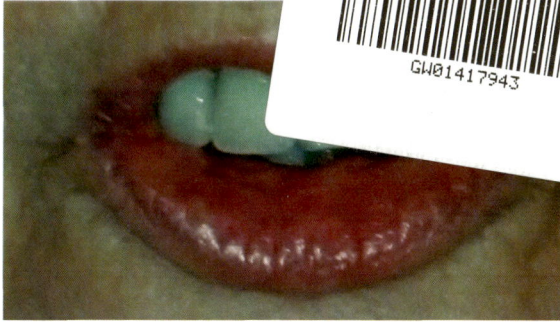

Voice

An anthology of stories

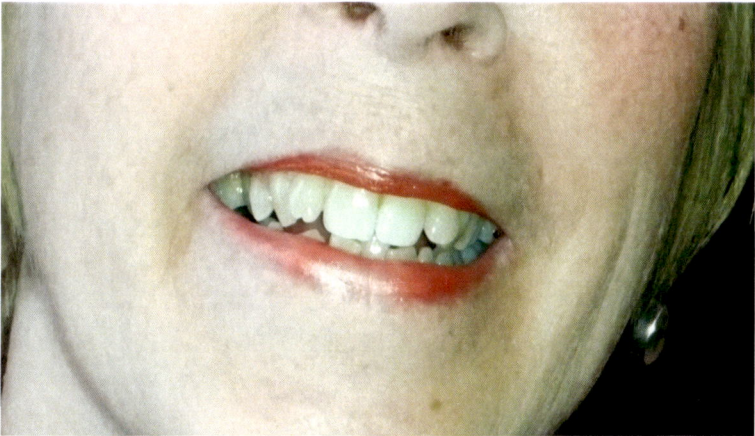

AGE
Concern
Carlton & District

VOICE

An anthology of oral

histories and

short stories

To Jim

Very best
wishes
from
Janet xxx
o/ Slack

Published by Age Concern Carlton and District
Cover design by the Print Quarter
Edited by Janet Slack
ISBN: 978-1-5272-1521-4
Registered charity number: 702763

Acknowledgements

We would like to express our sincere gratitude to Derick Ferguson (Honorary Secretary, Age Concern Carlton & District) for his ceaseless encouragement in producing this book, to Fiona Ellis Chadwick for inspiring the idea for the original stories, to Paul Hough for getting us funding for the website and giving guidance on the project, to Piotr Grzybowski for his tireless technical assistance on the first project and the book; also to the staff at Age Concern for providing the sandwiches and scones, our sustenance, and finally to Jackie Flower for typing up the stories.

Contents

Acknowledgements I

Foreword and introduction by Janet Slack V

Part 1 – Our Histories

1. *1934 And All That* – Shirley Ellis.................................... 2

2. *Behind Enemy Lines* – Freda Potts................................. 7

3. *Operation Overlord* – Pam Newton 13

4. *Life In The Meadows* – Christina Hale........................... 15

5. *Sunday Tea At Gran's* – Marie Hunt 18

6. *Some Enchanted Evening* – Kathy Hadrill 20

Part 2 – Our Stories

7. *The Sprites Of Elgin Smithy* – Shirley Ellis 27

8. *The Picnic In The Park* – Christina Hale 34

9. *First Airborne* - Marie Hunt 36

10. *Love Is All Around* – Marie Hunt 38

11. *Too Old To Play Games* – Kathy Hadrill 43

12. *Tom Pearson* – Kathy Hadrill 49

Appendix A - Autobiographies & Biographies 51

Appendix B - History of Age Concern Carlton & District 63

Foreword

This anthology was inspired by a theatre project which started in March 2014.

I had been working as a volunteer at Age Concern Carlton and District, Nottingham for a few months – sorting black bin bags full of clothes and odds and sods, pricing sale items for the shop, and generally just trying to be useful.

I had felt for some time that I would like to be more involved with the people who attended the day centre. This came from the fact that my older sister had been brain damaged quite some years previously and lived in a care home, a good care home where there were varied activities to keep people engaged. It had really helped her.

The opportunity for such involvement presented itself in March 2014 when the then Chair of the Nottingham Arts Theatre, Fiona Ellis-Chadwick, asked if staff at Age Concern could think of ways to get more people involved in the theatre. The theatre had been running sixty-five years and needed a boost. I jumped at the idea, and could immediately see there was an opening for collecting oral histories which might eventually be put on the stage and thus involving people at Age Concern in a meaningful way.

With that grain of an idea, I explained a possible project to our "boss" Derick Ferguson and Fiona and set about drafting a publicity flyer to get people who frequented Age Concern Carlton, or the wider community, interested.

The flyer was duly printed and circulated, and by April, I had had discussions with one of the creative writing tutors at De Montfort University where I teach English. The project was beginning to grow. Derick and Piotr Grzybowski (the then Retail Co-ordinator at Age Concern) were very taken with the idea and very helpful, and there was always the incentive of tea, scones and salmon sandwiches from Julie Carver-Smith (Volunteer Co-ordinator at Age Concern) for such a time as we could get moving.

With the help of staff at Age Concern, particularly Shirley Ellis, we finally got a group together in July 2014 and tea and sandwiches were duly served, and the small group of seven began to write and read out their personal histories in the ensuing weeks. We had decided on a chronology from childhood to adulthood and every time we gathered in the upstairs room at Age Concern, they revealed more and more of their enthralling memories.

The ladies, for it soon became ladies only, were full of stories which we recorded. It also became apparent that they had great writing skills and seemed to be enjoying the writing tasks and the regular get-togethers. But I still hadn't hit upon a way of weaving the stories together for a theatre performance, though it was clear some of the women had a flair for drama!! Then, I had a breakthrough moment one Saturday in March, 2015. (Yes, the ladies had been very patient!!). As their writing was very good, they could just select one story each, we would pick a piece of music to go with the story and I could write a narrative to join together the pieces!! In addition, Fiona from the theatre had a serendipitous encounter with Paul Hough (Creative Workplace/Business Manager at Broadway Cinema) and together they put in a funding bid to have a website built where the stories were to be uploaded[1].

Eventually, sometime in June, we went to the theatre to rehearse. The performance was OK but, understandably, a bit ragged. Nevertheless, we kept at it – meeting, writing, recording, eating salmon sandwiches. And, after some networking, I enlisted the help of Nikki Burt, New College Nottingham, to create some short dance routines for the pieces of music we had chosen. One of the final year FDA students (Abigail Parsons) became the choreographer with five second year FDA students performing dances (see photograph "Autobiographies").

I decided we could use a style of a review – stories, music and dance - to tell the stories. New College Nottingham kindly allowed us to use one of their theatres for the performance. (Sadly, The Arts Theatre was now unavailable.) And we started to publicise the event. We rehearsed hard and the day of the performance arrived, November 4th 2015. We had seven stories to tell and five performers. To cut to the chase, it was a huge success - a full theatre, great performances and bubbly and canapés to follow.

It had been a long journey but we all enjoyed it immensely.[2]

---

[1] Available on www.mystorymysteps.co.uk

[2] Performance available on:
https://drive.google.com/file/d/0B_RURy6yy3pRVzJyT1BDTlJENGs/view?usp=sharing

From that evening, the ladies have independently gone on to entertain many people at various venues in Nottingham. In addition, they decided they wanted to continue meeting and writing, so that we have done.

Janet Slack, Project Co-ordinator

JSlack - November 2017

Introduction

Like Sheherezade in *One Thousand and One Nights*, we
each have a thousand and one tales to tell. I'm not
saying these are tales to keep us alive: rather, that
people like to tell and listen to them, and that telling
sustains those memories and makes our histories
meaningful to our families and friends, and to those who
care to read them. Some of those stories are fresh and
illuminated, as if 1944 were now; some lie hidden in the
crevices of our mind, perhaps afraid to be dragged to the
surface; some are full of fun and laughter, like the smiles
and giggles of young children; some are sad, like the loss
of a loved one; and some are passionate, like the touch
and taste of a first kiss. Whatever they are, they are
woven into the tapestry of our lives.

Then there are the tales which are not particularly about
our life - pure imagination with maybe fragments of
conversations overheard, or scenes that we glimpse as
they dart in our mind's eye. They say that part of what it
means to be human is to create, and those stories tell as
much about us as the autobiographical detail and give us
a voice.

In this short anthology, there are the two types of story,
both a rich inheritance for family and friends to savour.
The first group of stories are the real histories from the
performance and the second group are ones the women
have chosen from what they have written for our creative
writing group and ones they were just inspired to write
before the group even started.

Co-operation, patience, commitment and salmon sandwiches have paid off. I would encourage others to have a go and see what beautiful writing can be created, and what friendships emerge.
Dear readers, enjoy your journey as we have!

Janet Slack, Project Co-ordinator

Part One

Personal histories - All our yesterdays

1934 And All That
Shirley Ellis

My story began on May 18th 1934 when I was born to
Leslie and Gwendoline Todd at my Grandparents' home
on North Road, West Bridgford. It was a very pleasant
Victorian house with large high rooms and a garden.
From here I was taken to a small, dark, terraced house in
Wallet Street, Netherfield with no garden. However, we
didn't stay there long as one morning mum got up to find
the walls heaving with black-clock beetles. So, we quickly
moved to 60 Forester Street, one of the happiest places
on earth, where my earliest memories are of being fed
Tarantella tomatoes, sitting in my own small arm chair by
the triplex grate.

My dad was a railwayman and had to work long hours for
a very small wage. Money was often tight, witness the
fact that we sometimes had to hide under the dining
room table if the rent man arrived before dad got back
from work on payday.

As a small child, I didn't realise that there were things
happening in the world, like the rise of Nazism, the
persecution of the Jews and the problems with our
royalty, which ended in the abdication of Edward VII in
1936. One thing I do remember though, were the bars of
chocolate in white wrappers with pictures of George VI
and Queen Mary on them which were given out for the
Coronation.

As I said, money was tight. We didn't have the luxuries of
bathrooms, indoor toilets or washing machines. We just

had a tin bath taken down from the wall and filled with water in front of the fire on a Friday night, an outdoor loo which froze over during the winter, a copper in the corner of the kitchen, and a dolly tub, "ponch" and mangle to do the washing.

As we didn't have any furniture in the front room I was able to use it as a playroom, until mum and dad saved enough for a new suite, covered in uncut moquette fabric, but we did have an old harmonium, which my mum used to play. At weekends, we would often gather round for a sing song with relatives, my speciality being 'Jesus wants me for a Sunbeam'. My mum had been in the Boots Operatic Society and also taught me to sing songs from Gilbert and Sullivan operas. I didn't realise at the time, but this was the foundation for my love of performing.

About this time, I remember a strange occurrence that has led me to think that there's more to this world than we know about. I went with my mum to pay a bill at the British Legion. I was told to stand by the table near the door, which I did, and talked to two little children who were sitting there. When mum returned I told her about the children I had been talking to, but they were nowhere to be seen, just the gaping hole of the beer cellar into which I could have fallen if they hadn't kept me talking. I like to think that they were my guardian angels.

Life was very happy and pleasant for me in the late nineteen thirties. I remember playing in the garden with the children next door, my dad making lovely dolls' houses and toys for me and days on the beach at

Mablethorpe with my grandparents. My grandfather was a true Victorian with an entrepreneurial spirit and was a clever engineer. I was allowed to play in his factory with washers and twirly wire from the lathes, no health and safety problem in those days. He had quite an influence on my early life. He used to give me pocket money when I visited and introduced me to the stories of Rider Haggard and Edgar Allen Poe, which were really quite scary.

However, all good things come to an end. Sometime in 1939 I remember everyone coming to our house for Carlton Wakes, which took place on the street. No problem with traffic in those days. After the fair, we were all in the kitchen when I was told to stay inside while the adults went outside to watch a strange green light which filled the sky. Apparently, the Aurora Borealis, or Northern Lights, could be seen further south than normal, but my family thought that it was unsafe for me to look at them. I have always felt robbed of this sight. However, much later I read a suggestion that instead, it was light reflecting off weapons that Hitler had ready for war.

At the age of five I was living in a country at war and school was on the approaching horizon. I rather liked school; there were new friends to meet and new games to play. I even enjoyed lessons and we were lucky to have teachers who were following a vocation rather than just doing a job, so they made lessons interesting and fun. We were excited at being taught how to put on gas masks that smelt of rubber and made your ears hurt and I also remember listening to air raid sirens so that we recognised them and knew what to do when we heard them. Although we had a lot of interrupted lessons, we thought it was great when the sirens went and we had to go into the shelters and wait for the all clear.

The shelters were another thing. As there was so little traffic, so few people had cars then, they were actually built on the street. We never used ours, which became a meeting place for courting couples and a public toilet, as living in Nottingham we rarely experienced bombing raids which would have necessitated us using the shelters. However, if the sirens went and things looked a bit dodgy, the boy next door and I used to sleep under the kitchen table near the fire, which was all rather exciting! However, I do remember being woken up the night the Co-op bakery was hit and the sky being alight with flames. I also remember watching the sky fill with hundreds of bombers as they got ready for raids on Germany and their return, sometimes in flames, as they tried to get back to their airfields.

 The war started to make an impression on me in various ways: young men I had known living on our street came home wounded from postings in Arnhem or the Baltic Sea, another chap became a fighter pilot and my uncle Harry was saved from the beaches at Dunkirk. We didn't always know a lot about what was happening because we only had the newspapers to inform us. Some people had radios that were run on batteries which were charged at the local garage. Everyone used to crowd around the set when Churchill was on and no one was allowed to speak which I thought was boring, but I guess he was a great morale booster. Our newspapers were full of reports of the sinking of ships and the number of aeroplanes shot down. I remember asking my dad what they would have to write about in the papers if the war ended. A very naïve question when you look at what is still news today…

Behind Enemy Lines
Freda Potts

The story that I have to tell covers a period of nearly eighteen months, from my flight to Paris in June 1940 to my arrival in Epinal towards the end of the following October. It was a time of very interesting, though sometimes rather unpleasant experiences.

The story of refugees fleeing from Paris has already been told many times. I think that the importance of my experiences is that they add yet another example to an ever-growing record of wartime German inhumanity. I have seen German planes on the highroad between Paris and Orleans, diving to machine gun defenceless civilians and dropping their shrieking bombs on us. It is unforgettable when you see a tiny child killed by the machine guns or another, crouching over the body of his dead mother. Those like me who witnessed these events will remember them every time we see a German uniform.

After the Armistice, I returned to Paris, where I continued my studies. I often planned an escape into a neutral country, but I took too long over it.

Early in the morning of 5th December 1940, I was arrested by the Germans. They were arresting every person with British nationality, regardless of their age or health, including women, children under sixteen and men over sixty-eight. The other men were already interned. Old people of ninety were forced from their homes, invalids were dragged from their beds, expectant mothers and those with new born babies were taken. I know of more than one case where a baby was born on the train, with both mother and baby losing their lives as a result. The Germans made no exceptions. It was absolutely disgraceful.

I expect that many people have heard about the camp for British women at Besancon. That is where I was taken, to an old French barrack, unprepared, filthy and infested with bugs. We used to hunt those bugs in the cracks of our bedroom walls with a red-hot poker. This seemed the most effective method of dealing with them despite the bugs only appearing to multiply with persecution.

The sanitary conditions in the camp were unspeakable, absolutely primitive and the food was so badly and filthily prepared that it was practically inedible. I think all internees feel very grateful to the Red Cross, British, Swiss, American and French for their continuous and generous help. Our regular parcels and cigarettes from the British Red Cross were extremely welcome. We lived under these awful conditions for five months, during which time the death rate was very high. Between two and three hundred internees died in the first two weeks. Thanks to the vigorous protests against our conditions by the Swiss Red Cross, at the end of April 1941, we were all transferred to Vittel, situated approximately 30 miles east of Epinal. Here our quarters were much more suitable. What a relief it was to be clean once more and to have seen the last of the bugs and the straw mattresses!

Despite the improvements, the spirits of the internees seemed to sink lower and lower. Anyone who has been locked up in a camp will know how gradually, but terribly, boredom takes hold of you. It is difficult to fight against. You seem to lack the courage to find an occupation or attempt to concentrate on anything. As our conditions improved, giving us less to worry about, we grew more depressed and our craving for freedom became even greater.

We gave our German captors a little trouble from time to time, for we were not afraid to voice our complaints. One internee, who urged a suggestion to our Commandant in the name of the majority, received the reply, 'Here you are not in a rotten democracy, but in a Nazi camp. You will do what you are told!' Although a lot more could be said about the experience of being in camp, I will pass over it and tell you instead about my flight.

I had always had the idea of escape at the back of my mind. So, I spent much of my time at camp painting watercolour portraits of my fellow internees in order to earn enough money to do so.

As the winter of 1941 drew on, I decided I could wait no longer. So, I forged a French identity card on a piece of drawing paper in Indian ink. One day I slipped off through the barbed wire. I can assure you it was a most peculiar sensation being at liberty again after eleven long months. I had forgotten what it felt like to walk around freely. I must admit that I was very scared because my capture would have probably resulted in being sent to Germany, a country that I had no current desire to visit.

Once out of camp I walked some miles to get away from Vittel. I knew that the Germans would not discover my disappearance until roll call the next morning. I had not cut the barbed wire especially for this reason. I was carrying a little attaché case containing mainly food for the journey. When I finally arrived at a railway station, I found that there was no train going in the right direction for two days, so I had to continue for a day on foot. I travelled by devious routes for the next three days, sometimes by train, other times by bus.

The whole way I was helped by the French people. Never once did they refuse me anything, even though the penalty for them, if caught giving help to a British fugitive, was death. I had left camp with 2000 French francs and arrived in Switzerland with nearly the same sum, because I had only needed to spend money on my train and bus fares. Whenever I pressed kind people to accept money for their hospitality, it was invariably refused. Their usual comments were, 'We are proud and honoured to be able to help England in any way possible.' I feel sure that every man, woman and child in occupied France fervently admired Great Britain and her allies, putting their whole faith and trust in us.

The last part of my journey was the most thrilling of all. A young French Gaullist offered to guide me over the mountains. So, we set out over the wide deserted woodlands to get to the frontier. We were muffled in a thick mist; the only sounds, the occasional clank of a sheep bell or the cry of a bird. Nothing broke the monotony of the moor, except for an occasional stone wall or large boulders and scattered sheep bones. I think all borderlands are equally eerie because they are so wild and deserted.

Before dawn on the fourth day after I left camp, we climbed the mountains to the frontier. Even up there the early snow was half melted in the November thaw and the pine trees dripped continually on us. My guide knew every path controlled by the Germans and we arrived at the frontier without meeting a soul.

The sun rose as I stepped into Switzerland. It was almost symbolical because at last I felt free from the Germans. Ten months later, I set off by rail on my way to Lisbon. The journey through unoccupied France was quickly over and the day after my departure I arrived in Spain.

In Spain conditions were bad. Those with money could buy anything they liked, while millions of poor folk had nothing, not even bread, for months at a time. I gave my sandwiches away to the railway porters in the frontier town of Port Bou. They took them with gratitude quite out of proportion to the quality and quantity of the sandwiches. In common with other Spanish towns that I passed through, Port Bou was half razed to the ground. In the devastated areas the ruins just remained, not rebuilt, not even demolished. Although ten years had passed since the end of the Spanish Civil War, there was still neither man power nor money to rebuild the wrecked towns. The streets held an abundance of beggars and evidence of poverty and hunger could be seen everywhere. It seemed sad that such a dreadful war had taken place in this beautiful country.

Travelling in Spain was very difficult. The trains were few, irregular and absolutely packed. They were also extremely dirty. Even in the first-class carriages you were tempted to put a newspaper on the seat before venturing to sit on it. Plain clothes men controlled papers on every train. I could speak no Spanish, but a lot of people, especially east of Barcelona could speak French. One woman said to me, 'I wish I could come to England too. You have bread to eat there!'

On the fifth day of my journey I arrived in Portugal. I saw straight away that opinion towards the English was very favourable, a tradition dating from the time of Napoleon. In Portugal you would have barely known that there was a war on. The streets were brightly lit and there was no rationing either of food or clothes.

I had to wait in Lisbon for four weeks until could get a seat on a plane home. It was a great feeling stepping off the plane onto English soil after three years away. I was so impressed to see how calmly and normally England was carrying on under wartime conditions. On arriving in London my admiration and surprise grew. There seemed amazingly little change even after three terrible years except that there were now more men and women in uniform.

I realised then that the English people really are unshakeable and that with this quality alone we could and would win the war.

Operation Overlord
Pam Newton

As the clock on the Prudential struck, I received my call-up papers. I was thrilled to bits as my mum wouldn't have approved if I'd volunteered. I was just nineteen. Off I went to Sutton Coldfield for three weeks for basic training. It was quite exciting and we also got to go to the dances on Saturday nights. One dance had to be cancelled, however, as the Colonel died, so we had to learn the slow march instead!

After the training in Sutton Coldfield, we were sent to Oswestry where I was trained in the art of height- finding for Ack Ack guns. This took six weeks after which I went to Wales to learn how to use the range finders for guns. It was very exciting, but also very damp as it never stopped raining in Wales.

Once I was fully trained I was sent to Felixstowe where I had my first contact with the Americans. They were very proper and well behaved. I remember they invited us to their cottage on the beach which had a sign saying, 'Happy Christmas to the ATS'. They had demerara sugar which we had never seen before and my friend made demerara sandwiches. We were taken by some of the soldiers to see the huge American bombers which were soon to take part in 'Operation Overlord'.

'Operation Overlord' was the code name for the Battle of Normandy, the allied operation that launched the successful invasion of German – occupied Western

Europe during World War II. The operation commenced on 6th June 1944 with the Normandy Landings.

As we were in the flight path for the German bombers making for London, we were on constant call. We would shoot down enemy aircraft during the D-Day Landings.

I was coming home from leave and had to walk from the station at 5:30 am with bombers going over me in droves towards France. I felt very alone until I saw a Bethesda church which reminded me of my mum and quelled my fears. When I got back to the camp, I made a hot drink and put a brick on the stove ready to warm my bed. I went to bed with a prayer on my lips for all of the soldiers going to fight.

Life in The Meadows
Christina Hale

It was a harsh winter in 1947! I remember the snow and the fire which was kept lit in the living room, but it only kept us warm if we sat close to it. Many women had red, mottled lower limbs which were a result of sitting too near the fire. The worst thing was chilblains, which we had on our hands and feet. Putting our shoes on was absolute purgatory; we had swollen toes and heels, and chilblains also resulted in painful hands, making holding a pencil almost impossible. Going to bed added to the discomfort. The cotton sheets were icy cold as was the bedroom. Sometimes my mother took a hot metal plate from the oven, wrapped it in an old towel and put it into my bed to warm it. Although this helped with warming the bed, the chilblains on my hands and feet would throb and itch as they warmed up. Thankfully, our parents didn't subscribe to the new fad chilblain cure which entailed submerging your hands or feet into a chamber pot of urine!

However, we loved the snow and played in it all day. My brother and I were the most popular kids in the neighbourhood because our father, a welder, made us a real sledge out of metal. My brother and I had to share it. I took my turn in the morning and he had it in the afternoon. Everyone wanted to be our friend.

My mother worked at Players and this meant that we stayed with a neighbour after school until our mother returned. For some reason, mother decided to change this arrangement and gave us a key to let ourselves in. On one particular afternoon, I arrived home first and put my key in the lock, but it wouldn't turn. I tried and tried but I got colder and colder and my fingers wouldn't work. I remember sitting and crying on the door step until my brother arrived home from secondary school and managed to prize the door open.

The snow eventually melted and normality prevailed, but not for long! One day in March we were sent home from school because the River Trent was rising. We felt no fear; we were so happy to be unexpectedly out of school and were fascinated to see the water coming up through the drains. When my parents came home and learned of the imminent flood, my mother advised my father to take the furniture upstairs. He pooh-poohed the suggestion, claiming that any flood wouldn't affect us, but of course it did!

I was awoken during the night by a lot of banging and crashing and few expletives. My parents were moving furniture upstairs as the water was already seeping in. This was the beginning of a 'topsy turvy' week in our lives. My strongest memories associated with this week are: being hungry and my mother donning her wellie boots to go to fetch food from the Salvation Army, the joy of seeing swans swimming down our road, and my brother sailing his boat and our neighbours calling out to each other from their bedroom windows. Despite the obvious limitations, I cannot once remember being bored – we kids could always amuse ourselves!

After the flood receded, we marvelled at the water marks on the houses and shops. Those poor people must have been devastated by the damage the flood had caused, but I never heard anyone moaning. I suppose they were pretty stalwart, having recently endured a world war. I will always remember the comradeship and closeness of the families in The Meadows.

Sunday Tea at Gran's
Marie Hunt

The letter arrived on a Friday. I knew something was
about to happen. When mam picked it up off the mat,
she gave a shocked gasp and quickly tucked the blue
envelope into the pocket of her apron. I slipped past her
up the stairs, went into my eldest sister's room, dragged
a chair to the window and knelt on it so that I could see
across the allotments towards the woods and the fields.
Our council house backed onto Broxtowe Woods which
was our playground, held secrets, happy days and future
terrors.

All was quiet, then on Saturday night my twin sister and I
were bathed and told that we were going to Grandma's
for tea.

"Why?" we asked.

"Be very good. Grandad is very poorly," was our reply.

In 1953, aged four years, being good was all we knew.
So, on the cold Sunday afternoon we caught a bus from
Cinderhill to Eastwood. We had never been to Grandma's
house before. It seemed dark and hushed as dad gently
pushed us forward into the room.

We cuddled together, two sisters both with pale faces,
light brown hair and blue grey eyes, shy yet curious.
Swiftly, silently, books were placed on chairs so that we
might reach the table. We sat side by side. I gazed
entranced at lemon tarts, scattered like sovereigns
amongst the ruby glow of jam tarts; pearly white bread
awaited golden butter; plump cherries sat proudly atop a

rich fruit cake, like jewels on a crown. I watched intently as tea, like liquid amber, was carefully poured into pretty china cups for the grown-ups. We were allowed a little milk in thick white cups.

Looking towards the shiny black range, with its two doors tightly closed, I saw the trivet had been moved aside. On it sat the kettle which to me looked like a large black cat warming itself by the fire. On the mantelpiece above was a collection of small bottles and scattered close to them were several small boxes. To the right in a dim recess I glimpsed a pile of neatly stacked packets.

Somewhere in the deep shadows a clock tick-tocked the passing time. From above we heard a dull thud and the sound of someone coughing. My sister and I started to giggle "Shhh", whispered Grandma. "Grandad Jim is awake." Everything stopped except for the clock and the hissing and popping of coals in the grate. Grandma and dad looked past me over my right shoulder. There was the sound of the door opening behind me and a blade of light pierced the gloom. I watched as a stooped, gaunt man shuffled towards the neatly stacked packets.

"Where's me medicine?" He spluttered between wracking coughs. He dropped into an arm chair, fumbled for one of the packets, took out a cigarette and lit it, his hands trembling from the effort of coughing. I sensed the atmosphere in the room change. Not once did he look our way. This was Jim Berry, our dad's stepfather and the first and last time that we saw him.

Some Enchanted Evening
Kathy Hadrill

The month was July and the year 1970 when the four of us travelled down to the west coast of England. The journey was, if I remember correctly, uneventful, apart from my co-driver, not just covering the clutch, but leaning rather heavily on the clutch of my car, during his turn at the wheel. Ouch!

In the summer of that year the Bairnswear Players had performed the musical 'South Pacific' at their usual venue, the Factory Ballroom on Perry Road, Basford and now we were trouping the whole company, the cast, props, scenery, lighting etc to repeat the experience at the Minack Theatre in Cornwall.

We arrived at the old hotel, set high on a cliff, in a very lonely area, as the heavy evening mist swirled around us, our only guide through the empty car park a pale, single bulb above the front entrance; the only sound, the clacking of the halyards against the masts of the boats in the harbour below.

As we entered the gloomy hotel and were led along dark airless corridors to our rooms, my friend Lesley and I, sharing, experienced a feeling of heightened anxiety and so we unpacked without a word. When eventually we found our way to the dining room I was deafened by the silence from our large and usually noisy group.

The meal was served and we stared in dismay at the pale and undercooked battered fish on our plates.

Whether or not I consumed that unappetising fare I know not, but I do remember hushed voices saying, "Pass me the ketchup" or "Where's the salt?"

Later, in order to lift our depression, we found our way to a very damp games room, where the old horse hair sofas had long ago spewed out their stuffing onto the ancient carpet and occasionally whilst the lads were trying to play billiards, frogs emerged from their dark and moist corners to frolic happily around us. No doubt they were delighted to have some company.

The following day dawned brightly and as Lesley and I, with some trepidation, went down for breakfast, we were not surprised to find the tablecloths were still stained from the previous evening, saucers were slopped with the beverages from the early risers and ketchup bottles displayed congealed rims, whilst the sloping floor encouraged tables to lurch ever so slightly towards the window.

The waitress, of indeterminate age, wore her dark, greasy hair in a centre parting and her crepe soled tartan slippers flopped loose pompoms as she walked. She had on a black skirt and a thin nylon cardie with sleeves pushed high up her arms. I'll wager her elbows had never been pampered with half a lemon!

"Now, my dears," she began as she licked the nib of pencil, held above her notepad, "we do have: eggs, boiled, fried or scrambled; bacon, plain or streaky; tomatoes and mushrooms, grilled or fried."

If someone asked for kippers or porridge she was really thrown; a nervous laugh and she would start again. "Well now, my loveys, we do have eggs, boiled, fried or scrambled; bacon..."

She had learnt her list very well, but seemingly could not just pitch into the middle of it. What she was called, we never knew, but we soon found a memorable nick – name for her.

There was one among us who had a quick temper, but he was very talented, so we had to tread gently around him, to keep him sweet. He, Ernie, wasn't really unattractive, though he was ever so slightly rotund, and suffered from sweaty palms, but the hairs sprouting from his ears and nostrils could be said to compensate for the sparse strands draped across his pate. So apart from a few missing teeth, he wasn't desperately unattractive. Consequently, for whatever reason best known to herself, "boiled fried or scrambled" fell for him.

When he arrived in the dining room he was escorted to his table, which displayed a crisp, clean cloth, sparkling crockery and cutlery. There were cardboard wedges underneath the front feet of his table to prevent any lurching. Then with varicose veins a-throbbing, she waited to take his order. I'll swear that if he had asked for a dish of lampreys from Botany Bay they would have been served. So, as he basked in her adoration for a week, he was as gentle as a lamb.

At last we arrived at the Minack Theatre in a wonderfully romantic setting and for anyone who hasn't experienced that magical place the visitor arrives at the top of the hill onto a plateau, having carefully driven his car up a narrow and winding road, he then walked down the stone steps to his seat. The stage was below him and beyond that the foam flecked rocks stretched out into the dazzling sea.

Long ago, the owner of Minack, Rowena Cade, together with her then gardener, created the theatre out of the rocks and she could still be seen every morning, wild grey hair uncontrollable in the breeze, mowing the grass in between the stone seats, whilst the sun blazed down on our troupe setting up for the show.

That year I did props and occasionally helped in the other departments. I also appeared briefly in uniform in the evacuation scene at the end of the musical.

The hampers containing the goods were housed in a dark and damp hut, out of site and below audience left and through the unglazed window we could see basking sharks below us in the bay.

I recall costumes taken out of hampers and hung on rails, especially rigged up for the performance, the chorus rehearsing on the open stage, electricians and set-builders shouting their instructions and the producer and musical director discussing the best entrances and exits for the whole show.

Anyone who knows 'South Pacific' will recall that the nurse ensign, Nellie Forbush, falls in love with Emile De Beque, a rich French planter on the island in World War II.

Nellie was played by my good friend Shirley Ellis who had red hair, a tiny waist and a belting voice and the gentleman playing Emile had an excellent singing voice but often misquoted the words, so we would get, "Some enchanted stranger, you may find one, er – twilight," or "The girl that I love is a guy!" All in perfect time with the music, so that we hoped that the audience wouldn't notice, though it rather negated any romance.

One scene that works well on screen but is quite impractical on stage is where Nellie is on in beachwear and under a shower, "washing that man right out of her hair." Then there is a mad dash for her to get out of her wet clothes (fortunately she was economical with the water) and into an evening dress, usually with help at the side of the stage – no time to go down to the dressing room – and then ignoring the sign that said, "Danger. Do not go beyond this point," she races down stone steps at the front of the stage, above the waves crashing against the rocks, to where I am waiting with heated Carmen Curlers to work miracles on her damp hair. That done, she races up the other set of steps on the opposite side of the stage, frequently stumbling in her haste so that I follow with a tin of plasters to slap onto her knees and hands before the blood shows through her white evening dress. She then emerges, unflustered, to sing, "I'm in Love with a Wonderful Guy." What a trouper!

On the first night, the gods decided they would join the action and designed for us a magnificent backcloth of a storm out at sea. The thunderous clouds and lightning flashes lent a wonderful atmosphere to our South Sea Island. They had even arranged for a small boat to cruise lazily around the bay.

On the Wednesday matinee, the rain teemed down and we were convinced there would be no audience, but right on cue they arrived and dripped their way down to the seats protected by large golfing umbrellas and comforted by trays of fish and chips, whilst backstage we were frantically cutting holes for heads and arms in the thick polythene bags the costumes had travelled down in. The show must go on! But then a little way into the performance, Aubrey, Shirley's husband, stopped the show, shouting, "This cannot continue! My wife is not a performing seal!"

Towards the end of the final performance on the Saturday afternoon, when the sky was a bright canary yellow, my friend Connie and I, both romantics, sat at the side of the stage and dreamed our dreams, gazing at the shimmering sea whilst we listened to the final reprise of, "This promise of paradise, this nearly was mine." Or did he say, "This nearly was yours?"

When the show was over we gave our many bows to the audience, then complying with tradition and out of respect, we tuned our backs to them and made our final bow to the sea.

Part 2
Our stories

The Sprites of Elgin Smithy
Shirley Ellis

The evening was damp and grey as the smithy loomed up out of a tree - lined hollow. The occupants of the ageing Vauxhall stared out tired and hungry. The journey had taken twelve hours and much as they were good companions, time and close proximity had caused tempers to fray. Unfortunately, the exterior view of the cottage did little to calm the situation.

The suggestion for the trip had been made at a quiz night in the local pub in St Ann's. Ray and his wife Joan had been best friends with John and Mary Thorpe for years. Recently, however, the arrival of an attractive widow in the area had caused some consternation. Not that there were any grounds for this, just that wives can sometimes have unfounded suspicions when their husbands get the 'working late' syndrome. So, to ensure that all was jolly and nothing untoward was afoot, a weekend in the Scottish Highlands was planned.

All went well with the planning; decisions regarding organising food and drink were made. Friday 12th October arrived, and Ray picked up John and Mary and the "attractive widow" Isabelle as arranged and headed for the M74 to Glasgow. The journey began in great spirits, punctuated with the usual panics regarding whether or not the gas had been turned off, the door locked, the lights turned out and the recalling of past occasions when these incidents had happened.

It was once there was a stop for coffee that the uneasiness began. Who was paying for the coffees became an issue. John was happy to get them but Mary thought that they should set up a kitty as motorway drinks were expensive and they were sure to make frequent stops. So, a kitty was agreed upon, but now how much to put in and who was to be the 'kitty keeper' became the next issue. Joan suggested £20 and that Ray should be in charge of the kitty as he was the driver. However, Isabelle only wanted to put in £10 and the men agreed with her, which didn't please the wives. Anyway, it was agreed, and the journey restarted, albeit with a somewhat subdued atmosphere.

On arrival in Glasgow, they piled into the nearest inn for a snack lunch. Now, the money issue got worse as £10 went nowhere. So, it was decided to scrap the idea of a kitty and everyone pay for their own lunch instead. This put Mary into a grump as the kitty had been her idea. She ate her meal in silence with everyone else attempting embarrassed conversation until John knocked a glass of beer over Ray's trousers and they all collapsed in heaps of laughter at Ray's discomfort. Helpful suggestions were made regarding how to dry the damp patches and after various attempts with tissues, Ray retired to the gents to use the hand drier.

At 2 o'clock they resumed their journey and while they were warm and cosy inside the car, the weather outside deteriorated with black storm clouds full of sleet and rain loomed ahead as far as he eye could see. So, a decision to press on with the journey with no further stops was made. This was not a good idea. As it became stuffier in the car, sitting comfortably on the back seat became more difficult. John was a stocky five feet eight inches and his wife a slim size fourteen. However, Isabelle was a well-endowed size eighteen, much of her endowment being located around her rear! There was not much room for manoeuvre in the back of the car and when the drinks consumed at lunchtime began to have their effect on bladders, things became even more trying. The layby they stopped in had no facilities, which caused no problem for the men. However, the women were anything but pleased as they squatted to relieve themselves beside the car in full view of passing traffic. Before they set off again, they decided that Isabelle should ride in the front with Ray, providing a little more space in the back.

It was now beginning to get quite dark and the roads were becoming more hazardous. Headlights from oncoming traffic temporarily blinded Ray on bends and precipitous drops from the side of the road looked very scary. It was getting towards eight o'clock and the village should be somewhere in sight. Fears that a turning had been missed started to niggle, when all at once a battered road sign appeared. Elgin 2 miles. Gratefully, they turned down the lane into the misty hollow to find Elgin Smithy Cottage.

The key was found under the mat and as the door opened, the smell of damp, unused space pervaded the air. A 60 Watt bulb hanging on a piece of wire lit the shabby entrance as they piled in and entered the small kitchen beyond.

"Where is the central heating?" was the first cry, closely followed by, "and the kettle for a cuppa?"

Ray, who had booked the cottage, looked through his pockets for the cottage information. This clearly stated that a fire would be lit for them by McPugh the local gamekeeper/handyman who would be there to greet them on their arrival at six o'clock. The few glowing ashes in the hearth were proof that he had been there, but as it was now nine o'clock he was nowhere to be seen. Taking charge, Ray delegated tasks. John went to fetch the luggage and food from the car, Joan went to make a drink for everyone, Mary tried to revive the fire and Isabelle went to check on the state of the sleeping arrangements. With someone in charge, things seemed to improve rapidly and once the log fire was burning brightly and they all had a hot toddy in their hands, their gloom began to dissolve.

Joan found space to store the food they had brought and was busy reheating the casserole she had made the previous day and brought along to eat with chunks of homemade bread. Mary had laid the table in the dining room and was busy exploring the rest of the downstairs space. She found a lounge with settee, two armchairs and an antiquated television and heated by an electric fire connected to a hotchpotch of plugs with a bit of exposed wire.

A shout from upstairs led them all into the little hallway, leading to the tiny bathroom which lurked under the stairs.

"What's wrong?" called out John.

"I'm not sure," replied Isabelle. "But I felt as though someone walked past me and I'm sure I heard the sound of heavy breathing."

"Don't be daft!" John answered. "There's no one here but us. It's just the wind whistling. We'll all come up and then you'll be OK."

So up the stairs they all went to choose where they were going to sleep. There were two rooms with double beds and a tiny cupboard with bunk beds.

"I guess there's no question of who is sleeping where," said Mary as she sat on the edge of the bed with a blue spotted duvet,

"Right …" said John. "Let's get unpacked, change into something more comfortable and get downstairs to eat that marvellous stew I can smell."

And that is exactly what they did. An hour later saw them sitting replete in front of a blazing fire with well charged glasses, an idyllic scene. But was it?

As is often the case when one is warm and well fed and watered, sleep soon began to cross our travellers' eyes. Ray suggested that it would be a good idea to retire to be ready for the adventures of the following day, which wouldn't be long coming as the witching hour was almost upon them. So, they began to make their weary ways to bed. The bathroom facilities were somewhat frugal, with only one loo and bath between them, causing a bit of a queue. So, it was well after midnight before everyone was settled and the cottage was relatively quiet, except for the deep breathing at various volumes coming from all three doors. If one listened carefully though, a more irregular sound, almost like panting could be heard coming from the smallest bedroom Mary turned over sleepily and was surprised to find that she was alone in bed. She hadn't heard John get up but thought that he had probably gone to the loo. She was far too sleepy, warm and cosy to be concerned. Then came an ear-splitting scream, followed by the silence of fear from the direction of the small bedroom.

"Did you hear that?" whispered Joan.

"Where did it come from?" came Ray's somewhat husky reply.

"It sounded like next door. Shouldn't you go and have a look?"

"Wait until I get some clothes on!"

By now Joan was getting over her initial fright. "Don't you think it's strange that neither Mary nor John have called out? And what about Isabelle?"

And then it happened. John burst in through the door, screaming with laughter but after a few deep breathes was able to explain what had happened. He had indeed found it necessary to visit the loo as Mary suspected and had had no difficulty negotiating the stairs. But when he came out through the bathroom door, a grotesque figure in white confronted him. Terrified, he had rushed straight upstairs and back into the bedroom, grabbing hold of Mary, or so he thought. In his haste, he had gone into the wrong bedroom and grabbed Isabelle and it was her scream that had been heard by all.

When they had all calmed down, Mary asked, "OK. While I accept your explanation regarding why you were in Isabelle's room, how do you explain the white figure?"

"I've been back downstairs to take a look," John replied. "We didn't notice when we came up to bed, but there is an enormous mirror on the wall facing the bathroom. That ghastly figure was me in my pyjamas!"

This could have been the end of the tale, but next morning, when Mc Pugh finally arrived he was very concerned to find out how well they had slept.

"Did you no have any strange noises in the night?" he asked.

Obviously, they related the story of John's nocturnal adventure.

"Och, I don't mean earthly sounds," he explained.

"What do you mean then?" they all asked with one voice.

"It's just that on the night of October 12th 1894 old Jamie McDougall died in the small room. He was 104 years old and very asthmatic. It's reckoned that he returns here when there is a full moon ..."

At this point Isabelle fainted.

The Picnic in the Park
Christina Hale

It was the day of the 'Picnic in the Park'. This event is a firm favourite of ours: friends Andrea and John, and Martin and me. However, I suddenly became aware of the sound of rain cascading onto the roof of our conservatory and down the windows. Oh, no! This had never happened before. Should we call it off? I thought of all the preparations we had made to ensure a successful day. What about the rest of our party that we had arranged to meet at the venue? As we didn't hear from them, we assumed we should go ahead as planned. Andrea and John were not deterred by the inclement weather and while the men busied themselves organising tables and chairs, we women concentrated on the food. Armed with waterproofs and umbrellas, we braved the elements with fixed smiles and dogged determination. Suddenly, the sky lit up with lightning and thunder rumbled. With heads down, we cowered in our car seats but pressed on regardless. Having parked the car, we squelched through the mud and rain, wondering if the others would be there.

Then the wind started up, I lost my footing and landed in an ungainly heap in the biggest puddle ever. With the help of the two men, I managed to get to my feet only to lose my balance yet again. This time I pulled my two saviours into the puddle with me. As the resulting expletives erupted, I felt mortified. With a little more help from other party goers we surfaced, but were all soaking wet and excessively muddy! We located the rest of our party and although wet and muddy, burst into hysterical laughter as did the surrounding observers. I didn't feel cold, and swaddled in blankets plus waterproofs and with my brolly I was determined to enjoy the show.

One of the acts consisted of four young women who sang with the aid of a microphone. This was entirely unnecessary as the music was so loud it vibrated off my ribcage. Gazing around, I noticed that many people had their fingers in their ears to drown out the noise. I didn't need to as I had so much water in mine!

The atmosphere was amazing – the wine helped! And the food that was salvaged from the rain was delicious. As the evening went on, the rain was still teeming, but our umbrellas saved us from the worst of it. The presenter then encouraged us to put our brollies up and down in time with the music. The laughter from everyone was infectious and not one person was deterred by the weather.

Suddenly, the rain stopped and the dark clouds melted away. We were then treated to the most spectacular firework display ever. Nothing dampened our spirits, regardless of actually still being rather damp!

First Airborne
Marie Hunt

David sat frozen with fear, his mouth dry. He dared not even lift his hand to rearrange the collar of his jacket. Keeping still, he hoped, would fool his companions he was OK. He glanced quickly at their faces. Each one seemed so calm, chatting, sharing the odd joke, even discussing what they would have for dinner that evening when they got back. "What if they didn't make it back! Oh, God! He felt sick with fear. Think positive, count, remember you're doing your bit. Think of those children. Remember, you're their only chance."

He remembered going into the sports club. It wasn't his scene keeping fit; cricket was about as close as he got to running and swinging his arms. If only he hadn't walked into him. Fancy walking backwards through a door! Talk about being in the wrong place at the wrong time.

Jean glanced across at David. He was very quiet, Was he alright? He had coped well at the training sessions. Some hadn't made it. Those who had, were now ready for the big one! She tried calling to him but he couldn't hear her above the roar of the engines, he was too far down the row. She recalled the night she had met him. He had been standing behind the door, apparently asking if he could use their phone. Her hands were full of tins and paperwork. She'd lent on the door to try and ease it open with her elbow when suddenly, it flew open. She staggered in, tripped over his feet, sending tins and paper flying across the room. He'd helped her collect them together, then over a drink, she'd told him about the work she was doing and the need for volunteers. David's friends thought he had become very secretive, even declining the chance to go on a weekend "sortie" with them, as they liked to call their visits to other towns and cities, but he was going on a special "sortie" now. The training was very intense and he had to keep a clear head.

Suddenly, he was on his feet. He was aware of Jean shouting at him and pointing. Next thing, he was standing with his back to an open doorway. He seemed to go on automatic pilot. He grinned, gave the thumbs-up to his instructor and was falling. It was incredible! The air rushed past him, forcing his face into a grin. He pulled the cord, his chute opened, momentarily, jerking him upwards, then he was floating, quite literally on air. He'd done it: he'd made his first parachute jump for charity!!

Love Is All Around
Marie Hunt

Miriam pushed open the door with her shoulder, clutching her bags and holding on to Whisper. A waft of warm air and stale beer swept towards her. Whisper, her chocolate Labrador, headed straight for the best seat near the log-effect fire which was switched on giving off a warm glow. He lay down, happy to lie quietly and listen to the sounds around him and take in the exciting smells of other dogs who had lain there before him.

Settling herself down too, Miriam put her bags near her feet, reminding herself what a nice pub this was for a mid - morning drink. She had been coming here for going on six months now. It was Whisper who had found it, one morning during a sudden downpour. He had pulled her in just as someone was coming out; the door was open so in he shot to get them both out of the rain.

"Hi Miriam," shouted Tracy, the young barmaid. "Hot chocolate is it"? "Yes please," replied Miriam. The murmur of people talking companionably helped her to relax. When she had told her friends of her weekly visit to the pub, they had been shocked and concerned for her. "You want to be careful going in there, it's a right dive, you know, all green 'n pink spikey hair, black leather, chains and body piercing everywhere. No manners. And the language! Jason who runs the place is an oddball too," they declared. But Miriam defended him and the regulars. They never bothered her, in fact they were very kind and Jason was a good landlord and stood no nonsense. Alright, she had heard the weekends got a bit rough, but folk deserved to enjoy themselves after being at work all week or job hunting.

Jason had been running the pub for over ten years now, Thursday was his night off when he handed control over to his head barman, although he was upstairs should things get too lively.

His partner Pierce was an interior designer. They had met at a Gay rave in the nineties. It was Pierce who had made sure Jason did not drink too much water but also made sure he did not become dehydrated. They had dropped acid together a few times, but all that was in the past - teenage kicks and all that.

They were happy to entertain friends. Pierce was a drag queen with bookings most weekends. He loved it, being very flamboyant once he had surprised Jason. It was a New Year's Eve lock-in, after Pierce had done his Doris Day Tribute songs he had gone back upstairs, got changed and come down dressed in Country and Western style jeans, red check shirt, cowboy boots and cowboy hat, then proceeded to sing their favourite song, "I love you because" by Jim Reeves. It had bought the house down. The locals had known all along they were an item but had respected their private life.

Coming through from the bar Jason looked around at his customers. He had quite an affection for them but he had one rule, in the week, folk who wanted to sit in the lounge had to keep the noise down or they would be out. He had with trepidation, installed a tea and coffee maker also a supply of those little biscuits in packets. He thought there might be trouble but to his surprise and relief it was a great success especially with the young lasses who could not afford Costas. Then he found out the lovely lady with her dog liked hot chocolate so he got some in. "Next it will be marshmallows," he thought, smiling. He twiddled his latest stud, the pain had almost gone from above his right eye where he'd had it inserted. He rubbed his tattooed arms and flexed his muscles. Hey well, he thought, it was worth the pain just to see Peirce's face light up at the thought of all the fun he would have mothering his "Jason".

"What you been buying then?" said Tracy, as she placed the hot drink carefully down on the table, not too close to Miriam. "Wool," replied Miriam quietly. "I'm going to knit a scarf."

"Knit! Do you knit?" Said Tracy. "My mums a knitter and a nutter." She laughed. "What colour will it be?"

"All different shades of orange and textures," replied Miriam. "The woman where I get my wool is very good; she helps me choose the colours. I thought if I've got some black left at home, I can make pompoms for the ends."

"Do you like my hair?" said Tracy, as if to change the subject. "Bright purple. And feel this;" she bent her head towards Miriam, who gently touched the spikes of hair. "You will ruin your hair," said Miriam, chuckling.

Tracy laughed. "That's what me mam said, but we had to laugh 'cos she's got none now, whilst she's on this treatment. I've put your biscuit at side of your drink. I must clear these tables."

Whisper's right ear gave the slightest twitch at the word "biscuit" and he gave a deep sigh of contentment. He looked at his adoring fans. "Aw i'nt he lovleh, Whisper?" someone would say, "Like the chocolate, the right colour too. He's gorgeous; I could eat him all up."

Whisper ignored them. But thought, why would anyone want to eat a dog.

Miriam drank the last of her hot chocolate and slipped the biscuit into her pocket then bent down to collect her bags, as she did so Tracy came over and leaning towards said in a stage whisper.

"Miriam. Do you mind if I ask you something?"

"Not at all," she replied. She was used to intriguing questions.

"How do you manage to keep all your different coloured wools separate?"

"Well," said Miriam, "I'll let you into a little secret: I keep them all in separate boxes with labels on telling me which colour is in each one. Now, can I ask you a question?"

"Of course." said Tracy, a little perplexed.

"Why do you shout at me," said Miriam. "I'm blind, not deaf. And the labels are in braille."

There was a deathly hush. Time stood still, Jason had been day dreaming about his night off with Peirce. They would slip their onesies on, open a bottle of Chateau la Mode and watch a boxed set of Holby City whilst feeding each other Jelly babies, bliss. He became aware of a change in the atmosphere. What was all that noise? Tracy and Miriam were rolling with laughter, holding on to each other, tears streaming from their eyes. Everyone around them was nudging each other and smiling.

"Now then ladies, don't forget the house rules," called Jason. But it was good to see Tracy looking happy again. It must have been a good joke. He looked at himself in the bar mirror, blew himself a kiss and smiled.

Whisper stood up as Miriam took hold of his harness. "Better get her home," he thought, "or that biscuit will be just a packet of crumbs.

Too Old to Play Games
Kathy Hadrill

Sydney, the old, ginger cat, settled down on the rustic seat. He curled his thin tail around his lean body, giving himself a measure of comfort against the harsh winter wind. All the time his light amber eyes surveyed the garden. The cold earth, naked and brown maternally guarded her secret, showing no sign of the splendour which would come with the spring.

Sydney was miserable with no friends to count on and not a place he could call home. His future looked bleak. Only this morning he had mewed pleasantly to the little man holding a rod over the edge of the pond. "Poor mutt," Sydney had thought to himself. "There's no chance of him catching anything with an old boot attached to the end of his line. Those goldfish are like lightning." Then purring softly, he had rubbed his bony head against the old man's shoulders. But the old man ignored him and continued to look straight ahead. "Miserable old sod," said Sydney. "I was only trying to be friendly." But when he saw his own image mirrored in the water below he couldn't help but think, "Perhaps people would like me more if I was handsome?" Gloomily, he returned to the old rustic seat and tucked his paws underneath himself.

It was true that nature had not been kind to Sydney. He was one of a large litter of kittens. The others being fluffy and playful, were crooned over, chosen and taken away to nice homes. "That one looks a bit mangy," one of the visitors had said pointing to Sydney's frayed ear. It wasn't crooked. No. Not even deformed, just a bit untidy, as if Mother Nature had forgotten to hem it properly, so leaving him with a lifetime of explanations.

Very soon he realised that his pale marmalade coat and white nose were not pretty and when he was only two months old, rough hands had left him in a field to make his own way in the world. Tiny and frightened, he was driven to hunt for food in order to survive. Consequently, he grew into a hard cat with a stubbly coat, sad eyes and a yearning to be loved.

A bird perched on the arm of the rustic seat teasingly close to Sydney's paws. He sat very still then suddenly swiped at the bird with a vicious left hook. But the bird flew swiftly to the top branch of the apple tree to smirk down at Sydney who began to lick himself furiously, hoping no other cat had witnessed his failure. "I'm getting too old to play games," he decided.

Sydney liked this garden and he liked old Granny Marshall who lived in the house which stood in it. On days when she wasn't visiting her daughter, Granny Marshall encouraged him into her home to sit in front of her fire. She was kind to him and gentle, but she wasn't at home now.

Sydney's hunger soon roused him into action and he made his way to the house across the road, where for the last few weeks he had enjoyed the scraps that had been thrown out onto the yard for him. He was never allowed into the kitchen here, which was warm and smelled nice. Once he had eaten, he was always firmly shooed away from the door. "He looks so scruffy and he's probably full of fleas," the lady had said from the kitchen.

Sydney had winced at that remark, but tried not to show his hurt. After all, it was she who had given him his name, the first he had ever owned. "It's a good sensible name," she had decided. "There's nothing fancy about the name Sydney so it's suitable for a plain cat." Sydney didn't mind her words. He was grateful for food that he didn't have to hunt and catch himself and he had made himself a nice bed in the corner of her garage which seemed to contain everything except a car.

The kitchen door was slightly open when he arrived, so Sydney waited patiently outside. Then looking into the room, he saw something which made the hair on his back prickle into a fin. There, inside the kitchen, eating from a bowl marked 'Pussy' was a black kitten and as it turned towards him he noticed with disgust the bright blue eyes, white paws and ruff of fur around its neck. He spat at it loudly. This was intolerable. It was pretty, pampered and worst of all, it was a *she.*

For Sparkle the kitten, her first view of Sydney, lean and tough, meant love at first sight. For the next few weeks she pursued him without mercy. She chased him, jumped on his back and chewed his good ear, for which she received a sound clout on hers, but undeterred, she continued to adore him with all of the passion of youth. Sydney, however, dreaded every corner he approached in case she was there ready to pounce.

"My scraps are getting fewer and she is getting fatter," thought Sydney bitterly as he watched Sparkle playing happily with leaves dancing in the wind in what he considered to be his garden. Suddenly, without warning she sprang at him and Sydney hissed at her. This sign of disapproval was meant to be fierce and intimidating. Instead Sparkle was delighted and jumped at him again, her tiny claws catching his sensitive nose. A resounding whack from Sydney's paw made her head spin as Sydney ran from her, past the little man still waiting for fish, and in through the half open shed door at the top of the garden. Sydney was just hoping to find sanctuary. Instead, as the strong wind blew the door shut behind him, he found himself imprisoned and alone.

Sparkle, who had witnessed everything, felt bewildered by this new game. She pawed at the shed door and finding it immovable, set up a thin wail. The light was fading and Granny Marshall, noticing only the kitten by the shed, went to pick her up and carry her inside the house. "Aren't you a little darling?" she crooned as her back door closed firmly behind

"But I'm your real friend, not her! She already has a home!" wailed Sydney, but the wind just carried away his cry. The dark came quickly and Sydney was cold. The only thing to sleep on was a sack, lumpy with potatoes. It would not yield into a bed so he flopped down on top and tucked his paws underneath him. "The old lady is sure to find me soon," he mumbled bravely although he knew in his heart of hearts that few people walk around their gardens in the winter. Then he thought of Sparkle sleeping on Grannie Marshall's plump knee and slowly two large tears dribbled down his thin cheeks and plopped onto his stubbly chest.

A whole day and night passed and Sydney was still in his prison. Sparkle visited and snuffled under the door, but thinking that this was merely another trick that Sydney was employing in order to avoid her, she flounced off home.

By the second day, Sydney had already relinquished all hope of release when the shed door opened and there stood Grannie Marshall with a colander in her hand. "Sydney! How long have you been locked in here?" she exclaimed. She saw his exhausted body, lying on top of the potatoes that she had come down to the shed to collect. He had no strength to greet her, so she carefully lifted him into her arms and carried him back to the house. She prepared warm milk for him which he drank while thawing out in front of the fire. Then she lifted his thin body onto her plump knee. "How did you come to be shut in the shed?" she asked as she gently stroked him under his chin. "I've missed you, you know. For two days now. And I like to have your company. You are my sort of cat. Sensible like. Oh, that black kitten is alright, a pretty little thing, but she wouldn't do for me, forever jumping on my polished mahogany and then running up and down the curtains! I'm getting too old to play games," she sighed. "Now my daughter has gone to live out of town I'll be at home most days. So, I'm wondering if, as you have no real home, you might like to come and live with me? I need a pal and I'll take care of you, then we can grow old together," She leaned her head back against the antimacassar as if waiting for a reply.

Sydney looked up into her kind face. He needed no time to think about it. So, carefully keeping his good ear towards her, he stretched up to rest his front paws on her shoulders and rubbed his bony head against her faded cheek.

Tom Pearson
Kathy Hadrill

"Tom Pearson," chuckled my old dad.
"I never saw a scruffier lad.
His ragged pants and scabby knees
Were souvenirs from climbin' trees".
"And in his pockets," said our mum,
"Were sticky sweets and chewing gum!"

Tom left behind his ways uncouth
And grew to be a handsome youth.
He was tall, strong-limbed and fair,
Wi' shiny shoes and Brylcreamed hair.
Admired by all his envious pals,
Adored by lots of pretty gals.

Tom chose his bride and they were wed
And there were many a tear shed
In chapel, as they pledged their troth,
Tho' folks were pleased and wished them both
Much happiness, good health, long life,
To Thomas Pearson and his wife.

The seasons passed, as seasons do
And gradually, the Pearson two
Became a Family of five,
When kiddies started to arrive.
So Tom could boast he was the dad
Of two little lassies and a lad.

'Twas in the autumn of his life
That Tom, cheesed off wi' naggin' wife,

Chose to ignore the mirror's truth
And thought to regain his lost youth.
Then he thought he'd try his luck
With Rosie from the Dog and Duck

He gave up pastries, booze and chips
And lost a few pounds off his hips,
Tho', his large paunch would not respond
To daily joggin' round the pond.
Nor could he hide the balding patch
Where once there'd been a golden thatch.

He told his wife he worked long hours
Then courted Rose wi' fudge an' flowers.
They danced and sang and laughed a lot
'Till his dull wife, he soon forgot
When he for comfort went to rest
On Rose, the barmaid's ample chest.

Now, Rosie was a pretty lass,
Her figure like an hour glass,
Enticed the landlord's handsome son
And soon the two were joined as one.
The shock proved fatal for Tom's heart
And from this life, he did depart!

When solemn wife and family laid
Their flowers on Tom Pearson's grave.
They could not see that for a while,
His peaceful face still held a smile,
For tho' he'd snuffed it in his prime,
My word, he'd had a damn good time!

Appendix A

Autobiographies & Biographies

Performance at New College, Nottingham, 4th November, 2015

Shirley Ellis

I was born in 1934 to Leslie and
Gwendoline Todd and lived in Netherfield.
I was educated at Carlton Girls' School
where we had some excellent teachers.
I began work as a laboratory assistant at
Nottingham University, but soon changed
to working in the British Plaster Board
Laboratory in Pilcher Gate. During my
teenage years, I was completely devoted
to amateur dramatics. I had a reasonably
good voice and just loved being on stage
and it was here that I met my husband
Aubrey. After I married, I worked for a
short time for Armitage Bros. in Colwick,
when we had our daughter, Fiona.

Very sadly in 1985 Aubrey died from a brain haemorrhage and our
company had to fold. I was devastated but fortunately, being an
addicted amateur dramatic actress, having some great friends, and
taking an Open University Degree saved my sanity and the arrival in
1986 of my beloved grandson once again gave life purpose.

I got involved in the story telling group through the Nottingham Arts
Theatre and Age Concern, where I work as a volunteer, and it has
caused me to remember so many past events, some good and some
not so good but all part of the life I am still enjoying.

Freda Potts (nee Moggridge) 1923-2017

Freda was an extraordinary woman who lived an extraordinary life. Always a bit unconventional, she'll be remembered for her sense of adventure, determination and as someone who was good fun. Born in 1923, the youngest of 3 sisters, she adored the countryside – fishing with her beloved father, Billy Moggridge, riding and exploring. Her one big disappointment was that she had been born a child and not a foal.

Freda excelled at School where she also first developed her love of art. Her teachers were keen for Freda to continue her studies after matriculation to try for a scholarship to Oxbridge. But art was her love and that was what she was determined to do.

So, she left school after matriculation and studied first with Cedric Morris in Dedham and subsequently with Fernand Leger in Paris. This move to Paris proved to be a defining point of her life.

In Paris Freda struck up a close friendship with Nadia, a Russian artist, and enjoyed her life in Paris to the full, perfecting her French at the same time. This was 1939 and times were troubled. But with that optimism of youth that things will be fine, Freda stayed where she was until it was too late.

As the Germans moved into Paris, Freda and Nadia fled South, cycling by night, resting by day. The sight of German planes firing on refugees including women and children stayed with Freda for a long

time. Freda eventually returned to Paris where she remained until rounded up and interned later in 1940.

Freda spent over a year in the internment camp at Besancon and then in Vittel at a Women's Camp. In Vittel, Freda painted portraits and was thus able to save some money to forge identity documents. In November 1941, Freda climbed through two sets of barbed wire, avoiding the guards and set off for freedom. Helped by the French Resistance, Freda made her way eventually over the Jura mountains to Switzerland, some months later returning to England via Spain and Portugal.

One can only imagine the bravery needed for a teenager to come up with this escape plan and then follow it through on her own.

Back in the UK, Freda joined the Wrens for the rest of the war where she met and married Joe Potts. After a short stay in Manchester and 5 years in Egypt, Joe and Freda settled in the South, in the Croydon area where she remained until moving to Nottingham in 2009.

With (eventually) 4 children, Freda mainly stayed at home to bring them up, fitting in whatever work she could alongside this. And she resumed her art, painting pictures when she could find the time with portraits providing another occasional source of funds. She also worked for a potter called Vera Tollow, cycling the 5 or so miles across to Vera's studio with one of her youngsters in a child seat on the back.

Joe died in April 1967 when Freda was just 43 years old. But Freda, resourceful as ever, quickly learnt to drive, passed her test and bought a car; and found a part time job at the Fairfield Halls in Croydon where she worked very happily for many years to come.

It was at this time that Freda returned to her passion for the countryside and walking. Freda walked over the years with several walking groups where she made many life-long friends. As well as weekly walks out in Surrey, Sussex and Kent, Freda was bitten by the bug of the long - distance footpath. In her time, she walked the Pennine Way (twice), Coast to Coast and Offa's Dyke (also twice each), Cotswold Way, South and North Downs Way, Glyndwr's Way and many others. If no one was available, that wouldn't stop Freda and she would go on her own. Glyndwr's Way, through some beautiful and very remote parts of mid Wales, was one of these solo trips and she was not afraid of being on her own. Where some of us might have had a quiet bite to eat and retired to their rooms in the evening, Freda invariably joined the crowds in whichever pub or guest house she was staying in making new friends where she went – and picking up one proposal of marriage from a farmer in deepest Wales!

Freda also developed a love of cycling. Again, this was triggered by wanting to reclaim a bike she had lent to her daughter Jo for a while and which was therefore in Nottingham. Rather than drive up and stick it in the boot, Freda decided she'd cycle it back down. "I can go down the Fosse Way," she said with a gleam in her eye. "I've always wanted to travel down the Fosse Way!"

Freda was very loyal to her friends and she would gladly give her time for them. When one of her friends, Julie, developed Alzheimers at a very young age, Freda would travel to Battersea regularly where she was in a nursing home to take Julie and Julie's dog Brian for a walk around Battersea Park.

Despite never remarrying, Freda had a wide social circle and enjoyed many activities. As well as the walking group, she belonged to the Croydon Art Society, the Croydon Open Group and the Gilbert and Sullivan Society.

Her schooling meant she could dig up a poetry or Shakespeare quote to suit almost any situation! She loved crosswords and in particular Scrabble. In her later years this turned into a form of speed scrabble. It's lovely to think that Freda managed two games of Scrabble with Jo the evening before she died.

She appeared on "The Weakest Link" when she was 79 and reached the final three before being voted off. To her delight, Anne Robinson roundly ticked off the other two remaining players for voting off "the best player." Freda loved writing letters which usually resulted in a reply and signed photo. She took a shine to some unlikely people sometimes. So, Tony Benn was pinned up next to Boris Johnson who rubbed shoulders with Bruce Forsyth and David Attenborough. All of them looked down on by Anne Robinson of course.

And as we all know, Freda loved cats. She had her first cat in the early 1980s (Sam Smith) and a number of others over the years – all adored by her. Her last cat, Miss Kitty, was one of her favourites and she was once overheard saying to the cat: "Miss Kitty, you are my favourite daughter!"

Freda moved to Nottingham in 2009, once it became clear that she was not able to live on her own. Freda enjoyed her weekly visits to her Centres, including Age Concern, Carlton, and had many visitors whom she considered her friends who came regularly to play scrabble, take Freda out or chat to her over a coffee. Freda moved into Edenhurst in 2017. Russell (who became another of Freda's pin up boys!) and his team did a wonderful job of settling Freda in and looking after her and she was very content in the home.

Pam Newton (nee Raybould) 1923-2016

Pam was born in Derby on 1st October 1923. She had an older sister Betty. The family moved to Nottingham and Pam spent most of her childhood years at Hereford Road, Woodthorpe.

Pam was called up in 1942 and joined the ATS. Her main role was a height and range finder on anti-aircraft (Ack Ack) guns. She was stationed on active service at Felixstowe. She watched troops depart at 2am on 6th June 1944 for the D Day Landings There was lots of cheering, then back to barracks for a cry knowing what lay ahead for the troops.

After she was de-mobbed she joined The Prudential, the 'Pru' where she met her future husband Ike. They had to keep their romance secret in the office until they were engaged. When they married she had to leave the office.

Pam enjoyed dancing, golf and socialising. When they moved to Carlton, she became a member at St John's Methodist Church in Carlton and was always very active within the church.

In later years she worked part time doing market research and she drove many miles with Tommy her terrier. Pam and Ike enjoyed many happy times at their static caravan at Sutton-on-Sea and hosted many visitors and friends each year.

Pam and Ike had two sons, Richard and Chris. Family and Friends were a very important part of her life and she was always interested in what her 5 grandchildren were doing.

Pam enjoyed 2 family parties at Christmas 2016 including playing with her great granddaughter Ada and feeling the 'bump' that was to be Ada's brother, Ernest. She passed away peacefully on New Year's Eve 2016.

Christina Hale

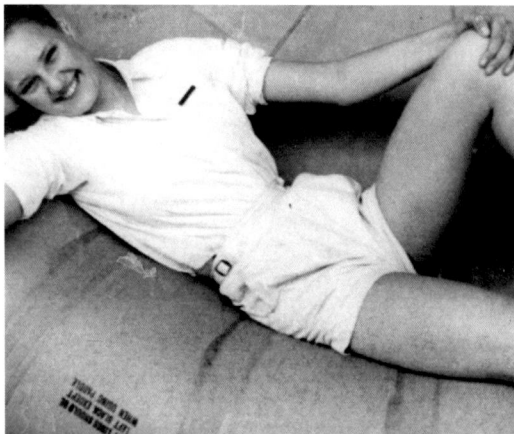

I was born in Nottingham City Hospital on 26th September 1938. My parents came from Melton Mowbray and I believe that my father had a sad start in life spending some time in a workhouse. My mother's parents split up, but in the same manner as much of my father's history, this was never discussed with my brother and me. We never met our mother's father and he was never spoken about.

I had two brothers, one older, one younger. Unfortunately, my younger brother died of meningitis when he was only eleven months old. Again, this was never discussed or explained to my brother and me. The baby just disappeared from our lives.

I enjoyed my education at Trent Bridge Secondary School and going to Pipewood for a month every year was an added bonus, giving me a sense of responsibility and the opportunity to learn about the wonderful countryside.

After I left school I was fortunate to secure a place at the Nursery Training Centre in Nottingham. I loved the challenge and gained great experience working in the different settings.

I met my husband on one of my many trips to Melton Mowbray. He was a dog handler in the RAVC. Unfortunately, he was shipped out to Kenya, to help fight the Mau Mau. From there he was sent to Cyprus where the EOKA, a Greek Cypriot nationalist and guerrilla organisation fought a campaign to oust the British. He was away for over two years, but we kept in touch and met up again when he returned home to England.

We were married in 1959 and moved from Nottingham to Farnborough. I secured a post as nannie to three children whose parents were scientists. My husband worked as a welder and we lived with his parents. Eventually, having had a daughter in 1960, we became the proud tenants of a council flat. After having two more daughters and moving to a council house, my husband heard of 'Big Money' to be earned on the continent. So off he went to Germany. Life was difficult for me at that time. I remember having to endure what seemed like endless power cuts plus the fact that the money he sent did not arrive regularly. The last time he came home he confessed that there was a new woman in his life and so he abandoned me and the girls.

However, I was invited to start a playgroup at the local RE camp. Perhaps the challenge was just what I needed. Another bonus was that I met my present husband and we decided to marry after a couple of years. That was forty-two years plus a son ago!

Marie Hunt (nee Wagstaff)

Marie (right) with twin sister Sheila

I was born in May 1948, the eldest by ten minutes of identical twins. The first three years of my life were spent at 41 Goodhead Street, the Meadows area of Nottingham. I attended Bosworth Nursery school until 1953 when my family moved to the Broxtowe area of Nottingham.

I enjoyed school but found it difficult to concentrate due to often feeling hungry. However, in my last year at Player Secondary School for Girls, I came top in R. E. In 1965, I left school with no qualifications.

In 1965 my sister and I went to see the careers' officer. "What would you like to do," he asked. "Work with horses," we replied. We ended up at a factory on Canning Circus, encapsulating electrical components!

I worked there until 1969 and during that time, met my husband, Peter. In 1970 our son was born, then in 1971, our daughter: our family was complete. I loved looking after our children; it was like a breath of fresh air.

Over the years we moved several times and I did different jobs, fitting them around the children's school hours. I cleaned for their teachers, the school governors, did "outwork", making boxed greetings cards and became a registered child minder. As the children got older, I worked in retail, eventually becoming assistant manager, though, through health reasons, retrained as a nursery nurse, then became a nanny.

As an adult, I've enjoyed going on different courses which I feel helped me catch up. I did NVQ 1 and 2 in Communications and Childcare, NVQ 1, 2 and 3 in Retail.

Many events stand out but here are a few: meeting my husband; the birth of our children, Philip and Marsha; the births of our grandchildren, Solomon and Samantha and on a different note, finding out in the early 1970's that some of us would carry the gene for Duchenne Muscular Dystrophy, but had no idea at that time what it meant or the heart-break it would bring. And to continue the list of memorable events: life-improving operations, two new hips, a phone call at work to say my house was on fire and coming home after a weekend away to find the downstairs of our house flooded!!

I have enjoyed many things in the past: youth hostelling, horse riding, campanology and now I enjoy art, learning the piano, hand bells, local and family history, gardening and volunteering at Shopmobility.

I got involved with Age Concern through my friend Jean who invited me to a meeting about memories and here I am writing my autobiography, to be included in a book!

Kathy Hadrill

My name is Kathy Hadrill, sometimes known as Katie.
I have always lived in Nottingham and for the first thirty something years of my life, my home has been in Gedling. As a young girl, I didn't cope very well with reality and so I escaped into my dreams which then opened up a world to all things artistic – performing in the amateur theatre, handicrafts and writing.
I was trained as a hairdresser, but I also worked as a waitress and barmaid, and then I was employed for many years as an advisor for a well-known confectionery company.
I have no children and remained single, from choice.
My sun-sign is Sagittarius, the Centaur, half man, half horse. The horse in me is probably a cart horse, plodding along, steady and reliable, but the upper half, the Archer, will always be reaching for the stars!

A brief history of Age Concern Carlton and District 1986 – 2017

(Registered Charity No 702763)

"Growing older is part of life and we believe that later life should be celebrated."

Age Concern Carlton was born out of the community which it continues to serve. Its inception was in 1986 when an appeal was launched for a mini bus to provide transport for groups of older people in the Carlton area.

The people behind this were Caryl Moore and John Mitchell of Age Concern Nottinghamshire and Derick Ferguson of Help the Aged. They were then joined by former Mayor of Gedling Cllr. Paul Newton, Rene Porter, Margaret Sherratt, Valerie Acton, Ken and Iris Johnson, Ken and Aida Palmer and Frank Giggins. They agreed to raise funds in the community, a philosophy which continues to this day.

The target of £11,500 was agreed and support began to flood in from Trusts, the Rotary Club of Carlton, local companies and day centres for older people. But most heart-warming of all, money rolled in from a volunteer-run temporary charity shop at 338 Carlton Hill, next to the old Co-op. The target harnessed the enthusiasm of the local volunteers under the leadership of Rene Porter, and they spectacularly raised over £5,000 in nine weeks!

The final sum raised was in excess of £20,000 and the minibus was presented in the last week of June, 1986. Most importantly of all, the local community had been galvanised – they had responded to the growing needs of older people! Such was the enthusiasm and empowerment that the following year, Age Concern Carlton and District was in the process of being formed, were seeking permanent premises and had enlisted the help of Don and Mich Stevenson, property developers, who facilitated the move to the current premises which were officially opened on 17 November, 1998 by Dora Bryan.

From the outset, the aim was to expand services for older people, and with the help of a bequest from Edwin Dawes, the "drop-in" became an integral part of this phase. Volunteers at this time included Barbara Holland, Doris Champion and Rene Porter.

We began to run regular coach outings to the coast and to distribute funds to local older persons' groups.

One of our greatest developments was to build a brand-new day care centre to the rear of the premises. This is now known as the Rene Porter Social and Activities Centre and provided Day Care that had previously been provided at St Cyprians Church Hall.

The Millennium saw Countywide changes in provision for day care. Age Concern Carlton and District assumed the responsibility for day care, previously delivered by Social Services as well as Age Concern Nottinghamshire. Since this time, we have continued to improve and expand our preventative services and to provide a lifeline to local older people. In 2011 alone, at the 25th anniversary year, we served 6.000 freshly cooked three-course lunches and provided 4.000 day-care place. Our "pop-in" offers regular companionship, information and signposting for advice and access to support for over 50 people daily, meaning 15,000 contacts every year.

In addition, our volunteers provide monthly Sunday lunches, outings, regular arts and crafts sessions and holiday trips to Bridlington, Eastbourne and Llandudno.

Our unique origins as a community- led independent charity continue to this day, with 95% of our income being generated by our own efforts and the direct support of the community, from which we draw a team of over 50 volunteers. Indeed, this book is the culmination of work by one of our volunteers, Janet Slack and the writing group (Shirley Ellis, Kathy Hadrill, Christina Hale, Marie Hunt, Freda Potts and Pam Newton).

As we approach our 30th Anniversary we are embarking upon our most exciting project yet! Led by our recently appointed Occupational Therapist, we are reaching out into the community to identify those most vulnerable and isolated older people and to offer appropriate support. We will be challenging the status quo and delivering innovative solutions as part of establishing an 'Age

Friendly Community' and models of good practice which others can hopefully emulate! We look forward to the future, confident in the knowledge that by listening to the older people we serve, we will be able to ensure that we are responding to their priority needs because ultimately that is all that matters.

Derick Ferguson, Founding Trustee